MW00618221

THE
CHANGE THAT
WE CALL
BIRTH

THE CHANGE THAT WE CALL BIRTH

Linda & Richard Eyre

Bookcraft
Salt Lake City, Utah

Copyright © 1984 by Bookcraft, Inc.

All rights reserved. This book or any part thereof may
not be reproduced in any form whatsoever, whether by
graphic, visual, electronic, filming, microfilming, tape
recording, or any other means, without the prior
written permission of Bookcraft, Inc., except in the
case of brief passages embodied in critical reviews and
articles.

Library of Congress Catalog Card Number: 84-71988
ISBN 0-88494-543-X

First Printing, 1984

Lithographed in the United States of America
PUBLISHERS PRESS
Salt Lake City, Utah

*Latter-day Saints
know who their children are, where
they came from, and what their purpose
is on earth. This perspective should make us
the world's finest parents.*

Contents

Preface

Eight years ago, Richard wrote a small book with Elder Paul H. Dunn called *The Birth That We Call Death.* The significance of the title, of course, is that in the Latter-day Saint perspective death is really a birth into the hereafter, a returning to God.

Ever since then we have wanted to do a related book, a book on the "death" that we call birth. For, in a way, our birth into mortality is a "death" from what went before, a temporary separation from God.

Because of Christ's light and atonement, both birth and death become beneficial parts of eternity. They become two great changes in eternity—two fascinating transitions in our journey toward a greater likeness with God.

The restored gospel gives us incredible insights into the change that we call birth. It allows parents to know that their children are actually their spirit brothers and sisters, totally dependent on them because of their tiny new bodies and the veil of forgetfulness drawn over their minds.

Latter-day Saint parents can thus view their own role as one of stewardship over God's children, and can realize that their handling of that stewardship will determine whether their families become eternal units.

Ponder the awesome title of *parent.* We know that in our premortal state we lived for a long but undetemined time as children of God. There we knew the being who had the title of parent—our Heavenly Father, God. In this moment called mortality we ourselves become, for the first time in eternity, parents. It is God's title. It is the title (*Father*) by which God asks us to address him. We assume that title and role here on earth, and we believe that we can keep it for the rest of eternity. The transition, in this life, from child to parent is one of the greatest role changes in our entire existence.

We know that our purpose in life is to become more like our Heavenly Father. Can any single thing make us more like our Father than becoming fathers and mothers ourselves? On this earth, there are some ways in which we understand our own parents only when we become parents ourselves. And our relationship with them changes because we now share their role. Our understanding of and relationship with our eternal Father changes in a similar manner.

These perspectives should have profound influence on our parenting. And with our unique perspectives come unique gifts and tools we can use in raising the brothers and sisters whom we call our children. We have the priesthood; we have the Church's meetings and programs. We have the guidance of additional scripture, ancient and modern. And we have the "absolutes" of commandments, standards, and values.

If you are a beginning parent (and indeed, each of us *begins* again with each new child) you will develop your own methods, techniques, and habits of parenting by experience. While we have written books on methods or techniques, this is not such a book. This is a book on *perspective.* We have written it because we believe that the best preparation any new parent can have is an understanding of what parenting really is, and of how it relates to the parenting of God.

Many books are written in offices, libraries, private studies, mountain or seaside retreats—in quiet, solitary, thinking places. Most of this book, on the other hand, has been written in our home, between changing diapers and paying bills. This seems appropriate, since God's children, at birth, come into homes like ours—houses where they are received by their brothers and sisters who have come to this earth a few years before them in order to become their mortal parents.

Perhaps a short poem can summarize both this preface and the purpose of this book.

The Baby Shower

Recent birth in the neighborhood.
Nothing is sweeter than a new baby,
unless it is new parents.
They are proud as punch, sure as sure
that history's premier human has just arrived.
I'll give them something—booties, perhaps, or a
    blanket.
What I'd like to give them even more,
much more,
is an introduction.
I'd like to introduce them to their own child, to
    have them meet
the reality behind this tiny, beautiful disguise.
"Parents," I would say, "meet your brother."
"Baby," I would say, "meet your brother and
    sister."
"Respect each other," I would add, "and
    remember
your true relationship and your shared Father.
If you do, you will serve each other in your
    common goal
of becoming as he is."

The
Change

Ponder a spiderweb.
It is constructed in such a way that large chunks
of it can be plucked away
with little damage or effect on the strength and stability
of what is left.
But within spiderwebs are certain crucial strands.
When one of these is broken
the entire web falls away.

Lives are like spiderwebs.
And the family is the most crucial strand.

1

Eternity and Change

A Two-way Eternity

We recently posed a question to a large stake gathering of parents: "What distinguishes the Mormon view of children and families from that of the world?" A vivacious young mother near the front stood and said, "That's easy! The answer is taped right on my refrigerator: *'Families Are Forever.'*" We asked how many agreed. All hands went up.

We love the revealed truth of eternal families. We enjoy telling others that our temple marriage ceremonies substitute the words "for time and all eternity" for the words "till death do us part." But is that our *most* distinguishing insight about children and families? Perhaps not. We have found that most religious people, in spite of the teachings of their official church theology, believe they will be with their loved ones in the hereafter. And despite their lack of knowledge of the nature of the celestial kingdom or of the eternal family, they have faith that relationships and love can outlast death. And well they should! To believe otherwise is contrary to the natural instincts of heart and mind.

Perhaps, to find the gospel's truly unique insight, we must look backward rather than forward. By definition, all Christian churches teach some form of life after death, yet (apart from offshoots from The Church of Jesus Christ of Latter-day Saints) *no other* Christian church, to our knowledge, teaches a life before birth. We are distinctive in our conviction of a two-way eternity.

While no Christian church other than our own teaches of a premortal existence, there is certainly some degree of individual belief. The experience of "déjà vu," the haunting feeling of having met a person or done a thing before, is almost universal. And no one, with or without gospel insights, has declared our earlier life with more beauty than the poet Wordsworth, who said,

> Our birth is but a sleep and a forgetting:
> The Soul that rises with us, our life's Star,
>   Hath had elsewhere its setting,
>   And cometh from afar:
> Not in entire forgetfulness,
> And not in utter nakedness,
> But trailing clouds of glory do we come
> From God, who is our home.

The Bible speaks in several places of a premortal existence, but its references, without the expansion of modern revelation, apparently are not specific or conclusive enough to take root in general Christian theology.

To be without knowledge of the premortal half of eternity is like being without half the pieces of a puzzle. To have that other knowledge-half is an awesome blessing that should have profound effect on how we view our children and our families. Knowing where we came from is the key to understanding why we are here and where we are going after death. Knowing our spiritual heritage is the key to correct values, morality, priorities. And knowing where our children came from and who they are is the key to succeeding as steward-parents and helping them return to their eternal Father.

Eternity's Two Biggest Changes?

God's plan of salvation for his children is built on the concept of change. The objective of eternity is to change ourselves enough that we become like him. Change is usually uncomfortable and often downright painful, but it is, in its positive sense, synonymous with growth.

During our eternal journey we develop and progress, often very gradually. But there are certain points in our course where dramatic, one-time changes occur that can catapult us in the direction of our Heavenly Father. Two of the most fantastic of these changes are the subject of this book. *Both happen at birth.*

First, when a child is born, he takes on, for the first time in eternity, a physical body like God's. Second, when *our* first child is born, we become, for the first time in eternity, parents, as God is.

In our eternal past, we have never before had physical bodies and thus have never been able to deal with physical matter as our Heavenly Father can. Nor have we ever before shared his role of parent. The first change (bodies) affords us the second change (offspring). The first change becomes permanent after the resurrection, the second *can* become so then, making the stewardships of bodies and our children gifts to us forever.

2

The Baby's Change

From Eternity into Time

Imagine what it might feel like: You leave the presence of Heavenly Father to go on the great adventure of mortality. You have chosen to go. You are a mature spirit, grateful and excited, aware of the magnitude of the opportunity to go to earth.

Perhaps the veil of forgetfulness drops slowly, in which case you may be "trailing clouds of glory" and "not in entire forgetfulness" as your spirit enters its tiny, helpless physical body. As the curtain slowly drops on the grand vista of your heavenly home, darkness surrounds you. Then a tiny pinprick of mortality's dimmer light appears. Perhaps it is cold in the delivery room, the metal instruments hard, the noise confusing and offending, the light stark and jarring.

You have undergone a change from eternity into time, from spiritual into physical, from galactic awareness into veiled forgetfulness. Tiny and helpless, you are totally dependent.

"It's My First Time Too"

A humorous story tells of a man, facing surgery for the first time, who lay on the hospital trolley waiting to be wheeled into the operating room. Seeking to calm his fears by talking about them, he attempted to start a conversation with a young woman who happened to be near.

"You know," he said, "I'm really nervous about this operation. It's the first surgery I've ever had."

"I'm glad you mentioned that," said the young woman. "But don't worry too much. You see, my husband is the doctor, and this is his first operation too."

Could there be an analogy here? We sometimes imagine our unborn children, looking down and anticipating their turn on earth. Perhaps as they worry about their trip into mortality they would not be comforted if someone said, "Those are your parents and this is to be their first try at parenting."

The story is told about a small girl who was sent one hot summer day to bring a lunch pail to her older brother who was at work digging a well. When she arrived, her brother was in the well and she could not see him. She heard his voice but saw only darkness when she looked into the black hole. "Shall I toss the lunch pail down?" she called. "No," said her brother, "hold onto it tightly and jump. I'll catch you, and we'll eat lunch together down here where it's cool."

A child, jumping into the black well of mortality, places his faith in the brother and sister who are to "catch" him—to nourish him, to teach him, to *parent* him.

"Perfect Love"

In Moroni 8:17, Mormon tells his son that he loves little children with a "perfect love." If any of us can approach perfect love, it would likely be with regard to little children. When we think of our children we are filled with a tenderness, a protective instinct, and a warmth. A favorite Eyre parent pastime is to lie in bed after a long day and talk about the cute things each little child said or did that day. We smile in the dark as we recall their bright eyes and shining faces.

Why is it so easy to love little children so completely, so perfectly? In large measure, it is because they are so dependent on us. They *need* us so much. This dependency kindles the deepest imaginable love within parents—and it may give us insight into Christ's total, perfect love for us. He is our elder brother, on whom *we* are completely dependent for salvation, for the light of his gospel, for life itself. In a lesser but similar way, our little brothers and sisters (our children) are dependent on us.

Dependency generates deep, charitable forms of pure love. The Lord has designed dependency into families so that love can flourish. Indeed, his whole plan is one of interdependence between his children. We depend on our parents, and later our ancestors depend on us to do their work and ordinances here on earth. And we all, together, depend on Jesus Christ and his atonement. Dependency creates love. And dependency within families is a two-way street. Our little children are dependent on us for their daily needs (including love), and we are dependent on them for the opportunity of assuming God's role of parenting and learning the attendant lessons that can qualify us for godhood.

So the change that a baby undergoes as he is born is an awesome one, as is the change his parents undergo at the same time.

Let us again summarize with a poem:

Two Fears

We remember well how one felt
but not at all the other.
One is young. The same age exactly
in fact
as our oldest child.
The other is slightly older than we and just
out of memory-reach.
Both were happy fears because a large measure
of anticipation was included
and we were, both times, following our own
   choice.
But the fear was real.
The first one, unremembered but revealed,
was when we stood high with God
looking down at uncertainty, change,
exhilarating, terrifying agency,
and at the inexperienced brother and sister
into whose hands we would put ourselves helpless.
The second fear, only twenty years or so later,
put us on the other end of the formula.
Parents this time to a tiny spirit brother,
knowing we were not ready,
hoping the real Father
would compensate for our weakness and
work through our fear.

3

The Parents' Change

Favorite Memory

We had been to the hospital earlier that day. False labor. But this was the real thing. As strong and intense as Linda's pain was, it was eclipsed by excitement and anticipation. What would this baby be? *Who* would it be? What would it be like to be parents? If our first daughter had been able to see clearly when she finally emerged into the world, she would have seen both of her parents shaking uncontrollably: Mother from the exertion of birth, Father from a never-before-felt combination of excitement, gratitude, concern.

The love generated by that tiny pink being was overwhelming. We felt proud, we felt moved, we felt frightened! We were still in graduate school at the time, and in student terminology we felt as though we had just gone from "Beginner Mortality I" to "Advanced Mortality V." Our lives to that point had contained the challenges of childhood and growth, of learning and developing ourselves. Our lives now contained the challenge of stewardship over another of God's children. We had actually begun our own kingdom; we had transcended childhood and become parents for the first time in our existence.

"Advanced Mortality V"

Imagine a thread that comes out of the sky to your left, passes in front of you, and continues off into the sky to your right. Try to imagine that it goes on forever in both directions. There is a tiny knot in the thread directly in front of your nose. To the left of the knot, the thread is blue. To the right, the thread is red. The thread is eternity. The tiny knot is this world, this moment called mortality. The blue thread is the portion of eternity you spend as a child before mortality. The red thread is the portion you could spend as a parent. It is here in mortality that the change takes place.

When the role changes, it is truly a shift from beginning mortality to advanced. Going from child to parent is like going from player to coach, from violin player to orchestra conductor, from student to teacher.

We give our brother-child a home. He gives us our chance at parent-stewardship. And we embark together on the greatest adventure of eternity.

To Everything There Is a Season

The early months with a new baby are a mixture of delicious joy and difficult reality. The baby consumes our time, takes away our independence and freedom even as he delights us and fills us with gratitude.

The blessing of having less time for ourselves is that we have less time to worry about ourselves. Baby replaces self as first priority. We begin to grasp the meaning of Ecclesiastes 3:1, "To every thing there is a season." This is the season of stewardship over children, the season to sacrifice many of our own wants and desires in order to satisfy theirs.

And it is comforting, as we struggle with this great transition, to realize that the change our baby has just undergone is even greater than our own.

Fulcrum

We believe
in a two-way eternity—
forever backward as well as forever forward.
We perch now on a moment of mortality called
     present,
the fulcrum between never-beginning past and
     never-ending future;
a pinprick of time in a vast sea of eternity.

But this is a *turning* moment.
On it pivots the meaning of before and the hope of
     after.
For here we change from spirit to soul
and here we change from child to parent.
Two changes God made deep-before
which allow us to follow
him.

The Perspective

*Perspective: The ability to see
from many angles; to have
vision, insight, understanding*

4

Perspectives from Feelings

We learn a lot about our children by trusting our feelings.

The spirit of peace we feel when we hold a sleeping infant and gaze into his angelic face teaches us that this child comes from a place of beauty and serenity. The discomfort and frustration of flailing arms and red wrinkled face teaches us that this is a mature spirit trying to fit into a tiny, uncontrollable body. The immediate comfort we can give by holding and loving as well as by feeding teaches us that we are responsible for the nourishment of spirit and of body.

5

Perspectives from Where We Came From

"He Could Be Me and I Could Be Him"

This is Richard speaking now, and I have a dilemma to share with you other fathers. I am a lighter sleeper than Linda, so when the baby cries in the night, I am often the one who wakes up.

Now, what do I do? One option is to pretend I'm still asleep and hope the baby cries a little louder and wakes Linda. Another option is to nudge Linda a little, hoping she will hear the baby and think it was his crying and not my nudging that woke her. The third alternative, which I sometimes wish wouldn't occur to me, is to get up myself and change a diaper or get a bottle.

I remember one night, some time ago, when I

reluctantly took the third alternative. It was about three o'clock in the morning. I had gotten to bed late the night before and I had an important business meeting with a client at seven that morning. I was not happy about the prospect of losing any sleep. I checked the diaper and (relief!) it was okay. So I got a bottle. Nine-month-old Joshua wouldn't drink it. I had now exhausted my list of things to do. He was fine (and quiet) when I held him, but screamed every time I attempted to lay him down. I walked into our bedroom once, hoping he would scream in there and bring Linda to my rescue. Linda was sleeping peacefully, and the baby didn't murmur. I considered pinching him. I tried the bottle again. No interest.

Enough time had passed now that I was no longer in that half-awake state from which I knew I could get right back to sleep. I was wide awake now, too wide awake, and I was getting angry. This baby wasn't wet, he wasn't hungry, he wasn't sick. What excuse did he have for keeping me up? I tried to lay him down again and thought his screams sounded like spoiled anger and not a bit like pain or discomfort.

I held the little fellow up, eye to eye, about to shake him or think of something to *do* to him.

And suddenly a thought hit me. It was a thought of *perspective*, of insight, and I'm not sure just where it came from. It went like this: "This is your *brother*. He and you were both mature spirits in the premortal world. You came down a few years before him. If the order had been reversed, he would have come first and been *your* parent. You would be small and helpless and he would be holding you up about to shake you in anger."

The thought gave me patience, gave me perspective, and saved little Josh from the results of my annoyance.

Interdependence of Parent and Child

Imagine the premortal world for a moment. There we all were learning of God's plan to send us to a physical world. Consistent with the presented plan of agency, Christ offered himself for an atonement.

Perhaps it was explained to us that we would start as tiny children with no memory of home. Maybe some asked why. We might have wondered why we couldn't go into mortality as grown-ups rather than as infants. Three answers may have been revealed to us:

1. You must start as infants with veiled memories in order to have true agency, to develop faith, to make your own choices and to start with a fresh, clean slate in learning to control physical matter.

2. You must start as infants in order to give other spirits (your parents) the privilege of becoming fathers and mothers and thus learning the lessons of parenting that will make them more like God.

3. You must start as infants so that mutual dependency will exist among God's children. You will depend on your parents for nurturing and training. They will depend on you for their education as fathers and mothers. Earlier generations will depend on you both to do their vicarious work and ordinances. All will depend on Christ for forgiveness and salvation. Through mutual dependency and a patriarchal chain of parents and children, God's family will become organized and governed for the eternity that follows.

And maybe there is a fourth reason. Could it be that the reason why babies can't talk is that they haven't forgotten yet and would tell us things we shouldn't know?

Agency and Asking

God knows that agency is an essential ingredient in the progress of his children. His commitment to our agency is total, so he does not take the initiative and interfere with our parenting even though the children we are raising are *his* children. The trust he puts in us is almost incomprehensible.

If we *ask* him for help, then he can give us help without interfering with our agency. When we ask, it is our initiative and not his. He *responds* to our initiative and helps us. We have used our agency to ask, and so he does not violate it in answering.

In England, there was one very quantitative, intellectual missionary who took delight in stumping his mission president. He came up to me (Richard) one day after a conference and said, "President, what do you think is the most frequent admonition the Lord gives us in scripture?"

I guessed that it was to love each other.

"No," said the Elder, "the most frequent admonition is a three-letter word; it is to *ask*."

When we think about life and stewardship from the perspective of where we were, the Lord's repeated advice to ask makes perfect sense. He wants to give and to answer and to help us in every way, particularly as we raise his children. But the principle of agency demands that his help come at our initiative, not his. Therefore, he asks us to ask.

The Greatest Perspective of All

Anyone who has had the blessing of a father who really loved him knows that there is no greater security in the world—unless it is the security of knowing that his Heavenly Father loves him, and that He *is* literally our Father.

Of all the *perspectives* we have through the knowledge of the Restoration, one insight is so important that it touches every aspect of parenting discussed in this book. It is the glorious and holy perspective of knowing that we are literal and not just figurative children of God. He *is* the father of our spirits. He is the *organizer* of our physical bodies, but he is the *father* of our spirits.

Understanding this fact and holding to it can give to us both the desire to be great parents ourselves and the confidence that we can do so—because we will have the guidance of the real Father of us all.

6

Perspectives from Where We Are Now

The Hardest Time in History

"Our children are disrespectful. They do not rise when their elders enter the room. They rebel against authority, they are more influenced by their peers than by their parents, . . ."

Who said it? Perhaps you did, yesterday, or maybe your neighbor. But the quotation above is from Socrates, and he said it twenty-five hundred years ago.

Have children always been the same? Has it always been as difficult to raise them as it is today?

We think not. It has always been a challenge, certainly. And as Socrates pointed out, children are children, no matter what the era. But we face some challenges and have some foes in the raising of children today that have never been present before. Four such challenges are:

1. *The "backwards priorities" of our society.* Perhaps more than in any other time or any other place, we measure each other (and ourselves) on the basis of our jobs and our possessions.

The media has duped us into thinking that women can only find fulfillment in a career; that staying home with children is menial, degrading, inconsequential work; so that a wife is not equal to her husband unless she does exactly the same things that he does.

We exist in the first society in history where too many live to work instead of working to live, and value *things* ahead of time, ahead of freedom, and even ahead of children.

2. *The pervasiveness and amorality of media.* Our children are exposed (whether we like it or not) to many kinds of voices. Many of the media they experience, from the lyrics of rock music to the situation comedies of TV to the "contemporary dramas" of movies, are either immoral or *amoral* in nature. Often the amorality (absence of concern about or of differentiation between right and wrong) is more dangerous than the immorality. The implication that "it doesn't matter," that "anything goes," that "there are no absolutes," that "it's the norm, so why worry about it"— these attitudes are subtle and insidious and they (in Book of Mormon words) "lead people carefully down to hell."

3. *"Big Daddy government" and "Big Momma education."* As the bureaucracy of government and education grows, it is far too easy for both parents and children to get the idea that government (and not the family) is responsible for the welfare, the development, and the learning of children.

More than ever before in the United States, for example, government and education are becoming the *masters* of families, rather than their servants. Governments tell us that children must be permitted to obtain contraceptives or have abortions without their parents' knowledge. The court takes children from parents whom it perceives to be unfit for the responsibility. Education defines what our children should learn and teaches humanistic philosophy in schools where prayers are illegal. And, for the first time in history, the average child is less well educated than his parents in the basics of language, science, math, and history.

4. *Social engineers and parenting "experts."* Parents keep getting the message in today's world that they are not qualified to raise their own children. Child psychiatrists and "experts" from all sides preach all kinds of permissive, analytical philosophies to us and make us focus on some complex notion of *understanding* children's behavior rather than on *affecting* and *improving* that behavior. Certainly there is much good advice in some parenting books. But at least five things are wrong with many of these "experts":

  a. They are great "complexifiers," making families seem impossibly complicated and difficult.
  b. They undermine parents' confidence.
  c. They all seem to disagree with each other, especially on such things as discipline.
  d. They follow whims and trends—some of the parenting fads of the sixties are now "the worst thing you can do."
  e. They usually approach parenting from a negative, reacting stance, saying, "If Johnny does this, then you do that."

What Should We Do?

As parents in the last few years of the twentieth century, we must have a clear perspective of where we are and of the negative influences that can affect our families and our parenting. We must say to ourselves: "The buck stops here! *I* am responsible for my children. *I* must be a greater and stronger influence in their lives than any of the other voices. I am the only expert on my own children, and although I will look for good ideas elsewhere, I will trust my own instincts and feelings. I will look to God and to the gospel for the help I need. I will take my perspective from the model of our Heavenly Father and not from the world."

One missionary friend used to quote a simple verse often:

> All the water in the world,
> No matter how it tried,
> Could never sink the smallest ship
> Unless it got inside.

When God tells us to be in the world but not of it, he is not asking us to be isolationists or to be unaware of or uninvolved in the world. On the contrary, the advice is two admonitions. The first one says, Be in the world. We should be involved, aware, participating—and we should encourage our children, as they grow older, to do likewise.

We should raise our children to live in the world. We should think of our families as riding on the world. *But we should not let the water get inside.* We should keep our families floating on top of and above the currents of amorality, permissiveness, and family destruction.

The first step in doing so is to have a clear perspective of where we are now and of the beautiful but confused world in which we live.

7

Perspectives from Where We Hope to Go

Quality vs. Quantity

We overheard a beautiful young lady talking to her nonmember friend about temple marriage.

"It's so beautiful," she said, "because it lasts forever. There's more of it, it's longer, it doesn't end at death, it never ends."

What she said, of course, is true, but only conditionally so. The *quantity* or everlasting length of the marriage will come into being only if the *quality* or beauty of the marriage is sufficient to earn it. We ought to think of temple marriage and covenant families more in terms of quality than in terms of quantity.

Sometimes we get the cause and effect backwards. Families do not become celestial because they go to the celestial kingdom. They go to the celestial kingdom because they become celestial.

Kingdoms

We are taught that our families are the potential beginning of eternal kingdoms. As we build our own family kingdoms, we are expanding God's kingdom— like envelopes within envelopes.

The patriarchal chain of family that is established here on this earth as one generation produces another will be forged and welded together by Heavenly Father and become his government and organization in the celestial kingdom.

This perspective can help parents greatly. We parents can think of ourselves as the trunk of a great tree. Our ancestors are our roots. Our children are our branches. We are the link between them. We must draw nourishment and strength from our roots and pass it on to our branches. We should learn of our ancestors, of their characters, their trials, their gifts, and their love. We should teach all of these to our children so they can participate in that legacy.

The popular television miniseries *Roots* illustrated what it can mean to children to know of their heritage and to participate in the strength and the pride of those who went before, those who gave to them much of their personality and their character.

In our family we have a big oil canvas painting of a tree. On each root is a picture of an ancestor. On each limb is a picture of one of our eight children. We also have a book of "ancestor stories," incidents of courage or character we have found in old diaries or heard by word-of-mouth stories. It is a way of keeping perspective, and of giving that perspective to our children.

Whose Goals for Whose Children

Many years ago, as our first two children filled our home with pleasures and joys, it dawned on us that we ought to have clear goals for our stewardship over them. Richard, as a management consultant who daily helped businessmen develop objectives, naturally felt the need for goals in the more important pursuit of parenting.

We began to ask ourselves, "What do we want to give to our children?" Over time, it dawned on us that this was the wrong question. The right question is, "What does *God* want for *his* children?" The right question is answered in the scriptures. God wants his children, in their mortality, to gain *joy* (2 Nephi 2:25) to gain *responsibility* (the whole plan of agency is designed to provide it) and to gain *charity* (1 Corinthians 13; Moroni 7:44-47). These last scriptures tell us that no matter what else we gain while here on earth, we are nothing without charity.

Asking the right question led us to write the series of books: *Teaching Children Joy, Teaching Children Responsibility* and *Teaching Children Charity.* Each is a method book suggesting that parents focus each month on only one form of joy, of responsibility, and of charity, and thus simplify their stewardship-parenting.

But this book is not intended as a method book. Though it contains practical suggestions, it is designed primarily as a perspective book. And perhaps the most important perspective we can gain is that these children are not only ours but also God's, and that we should pursue, in our own best way, his goals for their mortality.

The Feelings God Feels

A young mother expressed a feeling that many new parents have felt: "We recently had our first baby," she said, "and we were sorry my parents lived too far away to be with us for the big event. We finally visited them last week and it was wonderful. They take as much joy in our little son as we do.

"What was even more amazing, though, was the change in my relationship with them. As we were talking, I suddenly realized that something had changed between us. We were talking about the baby, and they were mentioning some memories about me as a baby.

"I realized that I understood my parents now in a way that I never could have before becoming a parent myself. We could talk in a way that we never had before. It was as though we were talking horizontally for the first time rather than vertically. I felt I knew them in a way I never had before, and I felt like we were so much more alike."

If we magnify these feelings, and put them into an eternal setting, we will catch a glimpse of how it may be when we return to our Heavenly Father, prepared to meet him again by the stewardships we have experienced here on this earth. To our great joy, we will find that we are more like him, that we *feel* more of what he feels. And it will be because we have become parents.

It Takes One to Know One

Understanding our parents
didn't occur to us when we were small,
and seemed about as likely as understanding the
  cosmos
when we were teenagers.
Different species, them and us,
we thought.
We felt guilty sometimes because no matter what
  we did

they never stopped loving us.
We wondered how that worked.
And we knew we were just as imponderable to
    them.
But mostly they passed their love down.
and we passed ours up.
Then,
they became grandparents
(we helped them do that),
and suddenly
we understood them and they understood us.
We shot love back and forth in a straight
    horizontal line.
Now think of God as a grandparent.

8

Perspectives from Scripture

Joy

> *He maketh the . . . woman . . . to be a joyful mother of children.*
>
> —Psalm 113:9

> *Children are an heritage of the Lord. . . . Happy is the man that hath his quiver full of them.*
>
> —Psalm 127:3-5

> *Rejoice with the wife of thy youth.*
>
> —Proverbs 5:18

> *Live joyfully with the wife whom thou lovest.*
>
> —Ecclesiastes 9:9

The scriptures tell us that families and children are to be a joy. They also tell us that life's purpose is joy, and thus that our goal should be to help our children find joy.

Joy is not so much the destination of life or of a family as it is the journey. Keeping this perspective in mind can help. Joy is an inherent ingredient in families. If we can look past the frustration and through the inconvenience, we can always find it.

Teaching and Training

And ye shall teach [my words to] your children, speaking of them when thou sittest in thine house, and when thou walkest by the way, and when thou liest down, and when thou risest up.

—Deuteronomy 11:19

Teach [sacred truths to] thy sons, and thy sons' sons.

—Deuteronomy 4:9

Train up a child in the way he should go: and when he is old, he will not depart from it.

—Proverbs 22:6

Adam . . . called upon his sons to repent.

—Moses 6:1

He that loveth him [his son] chasteneth him betimes.

—Proverbs 13:24

Withhold not correction from the child.

—Proverbs 23:13

Bring up your children in light and truth.

—D&C 93:40

Teach [children] to walk in the ways of truth and soberness; . . . to love one another, and to serve one another.

—Mosiah 4:15

And all thy children shall be taught of the Lord; and great shall be the peace of thy children.

—3 Nephi 22:13

Inasmuch as parents . . . teach [their children] not to understand the doctrine of repentance, faith . . . baptism and the gift of the Holy Ghost . . . the sin be upon the heads of the parents.

—D&C 68:25

Obviously, the Lord does not advocate passive, permissive, or reactionary parenting. The scriptural language is never, "If you have this problem, try this answer." Rather the scriptures tell us that the best defense is a good offense. We are to train up children, to teach them at every opportunity, particularly of the first principles of the gospel. We are to chasten and discipline them as they need it. And we are promised that, as we do, our children and our families will have peace.

Christ

We talk of Christ, we rejoice in Christ, we preach of Christ, we prophesy of Christ . . . that our children may know to what source they may look.

—2 Nephi 25:26

. . . that they may prepare the minds of their children to hear the word at the time of his coming.

—Alma 39:16

For we labor diligently to write, to persuade our children . . . to believe in Christ.

—2 Nephi 25:23

We need the perspective of knowing that the central thing we must teach our children is Christ. He should become the heart of *their* perspective.

After a fireside on teaching our children of Christ, a lovely woman came up and said that she thought the main thing she had done for her children was to tell them Bible stories of Jesus and then to keep Christ on their minds by putting a beautiful picture of the Savior in each of their rooms. She said the pictures were sometimes in between a poster of a rock group and a signed portrait of "Doctor J," but that she believed they always served as a reminder of what the children knew of Christ.

Taking a page from her book, our family now has seven different framed portraits of Christ, all of them personal "favorites." Each week the children choose the one they want for their room that week.

The point is, whatever method we as parents use, we must perceive the need to teach our children of Christ.

Prayer

Pray in your families . . . that your wives and your children may be blessed.

—3 Nephi 18:21

The Lord hath heard . . . the prayers of his servant, Alma, who is thy father; for he has prayed with much faith concerning thee.

—Mosiah 27:14

We must teach our children how to pray and we must pray for their well-being. This perspective is a simple acknowledgment of the fact that we need God's help.

In the mission field, when a missionary hears an investigator pray for faith and for testimony, the missionary feels a great weight lifted from him. The investigator has asked the Lord directly. Now the testimony will be able to come directly from the Lord, and the investigator will be less dependent on the missionary and on his testimony.

So it is with children. When they learn to pray directly to their Heavenly Father, he can bless them and nurture them directly. They gradually become more dependent on him and less on us, their earthly parents.

In the meantime, we must pray *for* them with as much of the faith and power of Alma as we can muster. "More things are wrought by prayer than this world dreams of," wrote Tennyson. It is particularly true with regard to our families.

Priorities

When a man hath taken a new wife, he shall not go out to war, neither shall he be charged with any business: but he shall be free at home one year, and shall cheer up his wife.

—Deuteronomy 24:5

In addition we are counseled to seek diligently to turn the hearts of the children to their fathers, and the hearts of the fathers to the children. (D&C 98:16; Malachi 4:6; 3 Nephi 25:6; D&C 128:17; D&C 110:15; Joseph Smith—History 1:39.)

The gospel teaches us plainly that our families are our first priorities. Even the Church is here on the earth as a beautiful but temporary institution to strengthen and give support to the *permanent* institution of the family.

The scripture from Deuteronomy quoted above might even indicate that we should be prepared to drop any other priority when necessary and spend full time in the home for a while when special needs arise.

There is no scripture that gives greater perspective than the one that appears in several separate places (see above) and underlines the importance of turning one's heart to his ancestors and to his descendants. If the Lord's people do not do this, the scriptures tell us, the whole earth will be wasted at the Lord's coming. Clearly we must work at this, in both directions, in this generation with our own children.

9

Perspectives from the Ultimate Parent

The Perspective

It is easy, psychologists tell us,
to model our parenting after that of our own
   parents.
Most people, in fact, do exactly that.
What is difficult,
but worth every ounce of effort,
is to model our parenting after that of our other
   Parent,
to father and mother our children
in the way God fathers us.

Seven Divine Principles of Parenting

All of us here are amateur parents. (Alvin
Toffler said it succinctly, "Parenting is the last

preserve of the amateur.") In the spiritual sense we are all beginners, offspring of a totally advanced and perfected parent. He tells us much, both directly and indirectly, of his own parenting, and he asks us to ask for his help in our own parenting.

We know our Heavenly Father follows his own counsel. We know he taught and trained us and then gave us the agency and responsibility to go forth on our own. We know that he and his prophets subscribe to the method of teaching correct principles and then letting people govern themselves. We know that his commandments to us are essentially loving counsel from a wise Father.

If we examine God's parenting closely we find seven aspects of his relationship with us, his children, that can have profound effect on our relationship with our (his) children.

1. *Laws.* He gives us laws designed for our mortal happiness, complete with built-in punishment for those who break them and do not repent.
2. *Sacrifice.* He gives us all that we *need* (not all that we want), particularly his Only Begotten Son and the Atonement that Son wrought for us.
3. *Plan.* He has a plan for us, called the plan of salvation. He does not leave our welfare progress to chance.
4. *Initiative-Agency.* Having taught us in heaven, he gives us agency so we can grow. He responds to our initiative with help and guidance, but gives the control and initiative to us.
5. *Teaching.* To the extent that we will listen, he continues to teach us always through his scriptures and his spirit.

6. *Availability.* His line is never busy.
7. *Communication.* We can talk with him any time, and he will respond to us if we have faith and if we listen.

Once when this list was presented to a group of parents in a regional meeting, a father came up afterward and mentioned that he was looking for a way to remember the seven aspects so he could be more conscious of his parenting. He said that, as he took notes, he noticed that the initial letters of the words, when put together in the right order, spelled PLASTIC. He said with a grin that he was going to go home and try harder to be a "plastic parent."

However we remember these points, and whatever we call them, they are the finest perspective of parenting in the world.

Perspective and Matter

We know so much, you and I,
of origin, purpose, destiny.
We know who we are and who he is, and
in quiet times, when spirit penetrates matter
and we see right through the surface and into the
    real . . .
in those mellow moments
we know that
family matters—
matters of laws and communications and family
    institutions—
become matters of highest priority.
And our children themselves, and perspectives of
    family,
matter more than all other matter
and all other matters.

The
Practical

I clenched my teeth earlier today, I nearly swore.
I slammed a door and shook one child
hard.
And I wondered what would happen if I gave up,
and I wondered why the whole burden had to fall on
   me.
There was one quiet moment in the afternoon,
kids at school, both babies napping.
I said a prayer and calm came.
I went in to look at them sleeping.
I felt a small reflection of God's parenthood
and I was the reflector.
And I wondered that he never gave up on me,
and I wondered that the whole joy had fallen on me.

10

Love and Respect

Ways of Showing Love

One evening when we were to do a seminar for new parents, some needs of our own children looked as though they would prevent us from leaving home together on time. So I (Richard) went on ahead to the meeting, and Linda said she would get there when she could.

When I got to the meeting and began my address, I felt impressed to ask the audience this question: "How does God parent?" They began responding and I began listing their answers on a blackboard:

1. He gives us laws.
2. He teaches us correct principles.

3. He has a plan for our growth and development.
4. He is always available.
5. He gives us responsibility and agency.
6. He sacrifices for us.
7. He is patient with us.
8. He intercedes when we ask and cannot help ourselves.
9. He watches us and is aware of us.
10. He gives us his power and lets us act in his name.

As we were working on the list, Linda arrived. I finished my talk and she began hers. She started by saying, "I like this list you have made of the ways God shows his love for us."

"Oops!" I thought, "it's not a list on how he shows his love for us. It's a list on how he parents." Then I looked at the list again and realized that it *is* a list of how he shows his love for us. I realized that, in its highest meaning, the word *parenting* can be defined as "ways of showing love."

Ways of Showing Respect

If we model our parenting after God's, then we look for ways to show love to our children.

If we understand the perspective of who our children are (our spirit brothers and sisters), then we look for ways to show respect for them.

We can show both respect and love for our children as we learn to:

- Show physical love.
- Follow God's parenting pattern.
- Practice the art of watching children.
- Think and pray effectively about them.
- Be children with them occasionally and learn from them.

If you are a brand-new parent, you may find some things to think about in the following pages —things that will help you form your parenting philosophies and attitudes as you begin the beautiful task of raising a family.

If you are already into the journey of parenting, perhaps these ways of showing respect and love will help you to further develop your perspectives and philosophy.

11

Touching— Physical Love

"Let's Finish Our Hug"

The first kind of opportunity we have for showing love to our children is through touch and physical contact. We have all seen studies about the mental and emotional importance of frequent, warm, loving physical contact for babies. There are also spiritual connotations and connections associated with this physical contact.

One of our boys was born nine weeks premature in England during our mission. He spent the first month of his life in an incubator and we could touch him only through the plastic glove holes in the plastic side of the incubator. When he was able to be taken out, we tried to make up for his earlier lack of physical contact. We held him all the time, we rubbed him, we kissed him, we fondled him.

It must have worked. Jonah is a loving, confident, thoroughly delightful boy today. Ever since he has been old enough to talk, he and his daddy have had a private tradition of "finishing their hug." Jonah will come and say, "Hey, Dad, let's finish our hug." They will then squeeze each other as hard as they can for thirty or forty seconds.

Baby Massage

There is probably nothing that small babies enjoy more than a gentle body massage. You can rub their tiny backs, their little arms and shoulders, their chubby small legs, and the pleasure and comfort they take in it becomes evident in their facial expression.

The massage can be gentle rubbing or it can be a light fingertip tickle on their bare skin.

As babies get older (approaching one year) they seem to like even firmer contact and enjoy being bounced a little, or tossed gently and carefully in the air. They also enjoy an occasional raucous moment or two of tickling and roughhousing.

12

Following God's Parenting Pattern

Laws

As they become old enough to understand, we should give our children laws, and children should perceive those laws as loving counsel from caring parents. Our family has learned three lessons about laws:

1. *Laws should be simple.* Our first list of family laws was enormous. We let every child make suggestions and we ended up with a list of twenty-eight! It included everything from "not plugging in plugs" to "not hitting little girls." A short time later, our oldest daughter made a suggestion. "Look," she said, "Heavenly Father just has ten laws; don't you think we could simplify?" We ended up with five, one-word laws: (1) order, (2) obedience, (3) asking, (4) peace, and (5) pegs. All but number five are fairly self-

explanatory. "Pegs" means that each child must get his or her four pegs into the family pegboard each day. One is for a family job, one for music practice, one for what the child should do each morning (be up on time, make bed, brush teeth, have prayer) and the last is the evening peg (go to bed on time, brush teeth, offer prayer, have room neat).

2. *Laws should have automatic, understandable punishments for violation.* The punishments should be as close as possible to natural consequences. For example, a child whose room is messy stays in it until it's cleared up. Children who are fighting must sit on the same couch together and think until each can tell you what *he* did wrong, not what the other person did.

3. *Allow provision for repentance.* With most of God's laws, we can avoid punishment if we sincerely repent. We should give our children the same privilege and learning experience. Repentance can be as simple (in its three-year-old version) as hugging the offended party, asking for forgiveness, and promising not to do it again.

Plans

In order to act rather than react to our children, we parents need goals and plans. As mentioned earlier, our goals should be God's goals of teaching our children joy, responsibility, and charity. At the beginning of each month, parents should sit down together and decide on one form of happiness, one kind of responsibility, and one aspect of service to work on with their children during the coming month.

Availability and Communication

We should learn to never give our children a "busy signal." When we brush them aside and tell them we are busy, we are in effect telling them that the thing we are doing is more important to us than they are.

Instead, we should take a minute, and take advantage of the teaching moment. If there is no way to do so, we should at least take long enough to say, "You *are* more important than what I'm doing, but I've got to do it right now. Why don't you and I go for a ride (or walk) right when I'm finished, and talk."

Teaching

Some parents see themselves as "general contractors" whose job it is to see that *other* "carpenters," "plumbers," and "electricians" get *their* jobs done. We drive our children from piano lessons to Scouts to school to Sunday School to swimming . . . thinking that *others* will do the teaching.

Not so! The buck stops with us. We should teach our children as much as we can ourselves, and should review and monitor as much as possible what they learn elsewhere. One good way is to make the dinner hour a time of communication and teaching. By having a regular time for sharing knowledge and feelings, we can establish communication habits and greater learning can take place.

Encouraging Initiative

The fact that a child's room is clean does not allow us to conclude that he is being responsible for his clothes and toys. The fact that his job gets done each day does not allow us to conclude that he is being responsible for his work. It may be that his mother cleans his room, or stands over him to see that he does. It may be that his mother reminds him repeatedly to do his job until he does it. For small children, this is fine and acceptable; it is part of the training process.

When a child approaches the age of accountability, however, things should shift more and more to his initiative. It may be helpful to have a pegboard system or a reward system where children fill out a slip each evening listing what they have done on their own initiative during the day.

Patience

Patience is largely a product of being mentally prepared for upsetting episodes. If parents would set aside one small moment each day to prepare themselves mentally, tempers would be lost less frequently. A mother might decide to think about the day ahead as she brushes her hair each morning; a father might pause for a few moments in the car before coming in after work. They might consider the types of irritation their children may present them with and decide in advance to respond calmly.

Sacrifice

Most remarkable of all God's attributes of parenting is his willingness to sacrifice for us. As we view our children as eternity's highest priority, we will sacrifice for them.

In the process, however, we should remember that we also owe something to ourselves. Pursuing our own personal happiness and fulfillment not only allows us to be better parents, it makes us pleasing role models for the *kind* of adults our children wish to become. One friend of ours, who we often thought spent too much time away from home—playing tennis, painting, learning to sculpt—ended up getting the last laugh. Her daughter, age five, was at our house for dinner and the topic of conversation was what the various children wanted to be when they grew up. When it was this little girl's turn she said without hesitation, "I want to be a mommy, because mommies have more fun than *anyone!*"

The Bottom Line

The best way, of course, to adopt any and all of God's parenting patterns or characteristics is to carry a question constantly in our minds as we pursue each day: "What would Heavenly Father do? How would he respond as a parent? How can I do likewise?"

13

Practicing the Art of Watching Children

Who?

We are funny, we humans. Those of us who live in New York City never go to see the Statue of Liberty or the Empire State Building. Those who live by the Great Salt Lake never swim in it. We travel to Europe or Hawaii to see things there and cross paths with people who live there, who have never seen the things we're going to see, who are traveling to see the things we live next to but have never seen.

We're a paradox. We miss the wonders of our own backyard. They don't seem special to us because they are common. They are so accessible that we can see them every day—we can, but we don't.

Now, it just so happens that the most interesting, the most beautiful, and most important things of all are right close to us every day. They are far more important than statues or salt lakes, and yet we don't notice *them* often enough, either. We don't pay attention to them and watch them and wonder at them and learn from them enough. *They are our children.*

What?

Pull back now for a moment. Let's review some of the truths we've already considered in this book: truths that need no argument, no proof; truths we inherently accept, most of us; truths that scare us.

1. Children are a massive responsibility. We shape their formative years. We determine to a large degree whether they will contribute to society or to its deterioration, whether they will be productive or destructive, happy or bitter, glad or sad.

2. We owe our children something. It was we who brought them here, by our choice. They are here because of us. Thus we owe them —we owe them safety, security, shelter . . . and we owe them love.

3. Physical parenthood is a capacity we inherit. Mental and emotional parenthood are not. Children are often hard to understand, hard to deal with. Parenthood is a severe challenge; it comes easily to no one.

4. The world is a tough place to live in, and it's getting tougher. By the time they become adults, children need some workable answers; they need to be able to cope, to handle problems, to make decisions.

5. Children are our own best insurance. As we grow older, children should be a key source of joy, of security, of fulfillment.

Could it be that the key to answering all five of these challenges, the key to successful parenthood, is as simple as learning how to watch our children?

Parents who develop intense interest in their children, who learn the art of watching them, will find that all the other answers are already there, waiting, just inside of situations, just inside of their children, just inside of themselves—waiting to be found by the parent who has learned to *watch.*

Where and When?

Let's delve a little further into this "watching" idea with a short question-and-answer game.

Q. Doesn't every parent watch his children?

A. No. All parents see them, but few *watch.* All parents hear, but few *listen.* All parents look, but few *observe.*

Q. What does watching mean, then?

A. Watching means seeing all that is happening, inside and out: watching with the joy and interest with which an avid sports fan watches an overtime basketball game, watching with the art and attention that a detective uses in solving a case.

Q. Doesn't that take a lot of concentration?

A. Yes.

Q. Isn't it tiring?

A. Yes, but it's also renewing.

Q. What are the benefits?

A. The mistakes parents make usually spring not from not knowing answers, but from not under-standing needs. A parent who sees a need clearly usually knows the solution. Watching reveals the real needs, the underneath needs, the places where help can really be given.

Q.   How does a parent do this kind of watching?
A.   Read on, that part is coming.

Why?

A parent who learns the art and discovers the joy of watching children will find five benefits, each one important, each one a key to many related things. Watching benefits the child in some ways, the parent in others; still other benefits extend to both.

1. A parent who learns the art of watching a child will understand that child well enough to be his true friend. Generation gaps, parent-child communication breakdowns can't happen among true friends, amidst real understanding. The art of watching children can make your children into true friends who trust, who share, who ask for and accept help.

2. Children who are truly watched by their parents will have a magnified chance of discovering and fulfilling their true potentials. Children, like acorns, have inside them the seed of all that they can become. A child's success is not a question of what a parent puts into him, but rather of what a parent draws out. A parent who masters the art of watching children will see all that is there, and will not see things that are not there.

3. The benefits of watching children are similar to the benefits of watching experts in any field. Children are experts at many of the things we adults value most, want most. Children are experts at spontaneity, at imagination, at creativity, at candor and honesty, at simple faith, at curiosity and interest, at trust and openness.

4. Parents who learn the art of watching children will learn to know themselves. They will see themselves reflected in many of their children's actions.

5. The great blessing of real observation, real *watching,* is that good is found in everything. Silver linings are always revealed. A nonwatching parent may see nothing but irritation and time-waste in a quarrel between two children that he has to settle and resolve. A parent who has mastered the art of watching will see personalities revealed, needs manifested, potentials displayed, and will find interest and satisfaction in the teaching moment that the quarrel provides.

How?

How does a parent *watch?*

It's an interesting question, an ironic question in a way. People usually don't have to be told how to watch something they are deeply interested in. I don't have to be told how to watch a football game. It comes naturally because I like it, because I'm interested in it.

Let's learn from the football watcher. If he watches naturally, easily, expertly, then we ought to see how he does it and attempt to watch children in the same way. What does he do? What is the art of his watching that makes his watching a joy?

There is a "before," a "during," and an "after" aspect of the football viewer's watching, each of which makes the watching more thorough and more enjoyable. Let's look at each:

A. *Before*
1. He thinks about the game, knows the statistics on the players, knows the

odds, knows what's going on behind
the scenes. He has *background.*

2.   He sets aside the time necessary to
watch the game, so he can go and see it
without interruption, without worrying
about other things.

The two together add up to preparation
and anticipation.

B.   *During*

There are two kinds of doing for the football fan. He has to do both to fully appre-
ciate each.

1.   *Watching*—attentively, intensely, with
natural, spontaneous, interest.

2.   *Doing*—he plays a little football
himself, maybe with his children, maybe with the boys; he tries the plays,
throws the passes, participates in the
game himself.

C.   *After*

He magnifies the joy and extends the art
by doing two things afterward.

1.   Talking about the game with another
fan, remembering and reliving the
highlights, thinking and speculating
on what plays should have been called.

2.   Writing about it. If he has the inclina-
tion, and if he is a *real* fan, he may
mention it in his journal, write a letter
to the sports editor, or just write out a
play diagram for the fourth down that
could have made a difference.

A parent who practices the fine art of watching
children follows a very similar pattern:

A.   *Before*

1.   He thinks about his children, discusses
them with his spouse, wonders about

their needs, goes to parent-teacher con-
ferences, gets all the background he
can.

2. He sets aside time; perhaps one night a
    week for the whole family to do some-
    thing together, perhaps a special one-
    on-one time to be with each child, per-
    haps some time to do nothing but sit
    and listen and observe.

B. *During*
1. Watching, observing, seeing motives,
    responses, needs, causes—*thinking.*
2. *Doing.* Watching isn't really *watching*
    until it is done from the player's level.
    The parent has to take off his shoes and
    stomp in the puddle *with* the child
    every once in a while.

C. *After*
1. Talking about it together as parents,
    sharing each other's insight, remem-
    bering observations together. Perhaps
    you discuss each child individually, his
    physical, mental, emotional, and social
    progress. Where are the main needs?
    How can you fill them?
2. Writing about it. Part of the art of
    watching children is to have a journal
    for each child and to record observa-
    tions regularly. The writing helps
    organize these observations, makes
    them official and demanding of atten-
    tion and follow-through.

So What?

Watching children, the joy and the art: What is
the end result, the bottom line? Is *watching* all there is
to it?

No, but the art of watching will lead to all that there is to it.

Parenthood is *in* us. It's not automatic and it's not always easy or natural. But it is in us. We have the insights and the instincts for it. Watching children, really *watching* them, is the catalyst. It is the pilot light that keeps our abilities as parents burning, growing.

The watching parent will see more than a child shy of participation; he will see a need for self-esteem and he will see opportunities to give it. He will see more than a loud, aggressive child; he will see the need for real attention and will see opportunities to give it.

The key is watching, the art of watching children. As with all arts, it is not easily learned. The "exercises" suggested next will help. Like any art, like any skill, the ability to truly watch children comes through practice—even through training.

The first prerequisite is the desire to gain the skill — enough desire that one will put forth the effort, through practice and actual exercises, to develop the ability, to master the art.

Here are three separate exercises to begin with:

1. *The focused hour.* Find an unobstructed hour, perhaps on a Saturday afternoon, perhaps a weekday evening, when you have no commitment, no dinner time, no interruption—and do nothing but observe your children. Observe with a notebook, writing down everything you observe. Watch and listen from a distance, without becoming involved with the children. Watch their play, their interactions, their facial expressions, their body language, their tendencies, their reactions. Listen to their

comments, their tone of voice, their temperaments. Take notes on everything you observe. Don't let your mind wander, not even to related things like when you will buy Johnny the new shoes he needs. As thoughts occur other than the observations about children, jot a note to remind you to think about them later ("new shoes—Johnny") and return your entire attention to simply watching. When the hour is over, share your recorded observations with your spouse.

2. *Single child focus.* Designate a particular day to watch a particular child. During that entire day, whenever you are with that child (at meals, around the house, in the car, at bedtime) focus your observation on him. What does the world look like through his eyes? Can you remember anything about being that age yourself? What is he thinking? What is he worried about? What is important to him? What are his natural gifts and inclinations? What are his securities and insecurities? Again, make notes of your main observations. Share them with your spouse at the end of the day.

3. *Making connections.* Try to fill in the accompanying question sheet for one of your children and for yourself, based on your memory of when you were exactly the same age. On any matter that is not obvious or quickly clear to you, watch the child carefully, looking for the answer, until one comes. See if discovering answers about your child helps you to remember the answers about yourself at the same age.

	1.	height, weight
	2.	school, teacher
	3.	strongest current interests
	4.	natural gifts, abilities
	5.	principal fears, worries
	6.	best friends
	7.	favorite activities
	8.	least favorite activities
	9.	personality traits
	10.	social and emotional traits

Your Child	*Yourself at Same Age*
1.	1.
2.	2.
3.	3.
4.	4.
5.	5.
6.	6.
7.	7.
8.	8.
9.	9.
10.	10.

14

Thinking and Praying Effectively

"You Took No Thought . . ."

We knelt to pray one night early in our marriage, following a particularly trying day with our three small children. Our prayer centered on our need for help as parents. "Help us to have more patience. Help us to understand each of our children." It was a sincere prayer, for we felt some real needs and concerns.

Yet instead of an answer, we felt something akin to a rebuke or a reprimand. What came to our minds was an echo of the Lord's words to Oliver Cowdery in section 9 of the Doctrine and Covenants. Oliver too had made a sincere request, but the Lord answered, "You took no thought save it was to ask."

As stressed earlier, the Lord asks us to ask. But he also asks us to *think* before we ask. Thought and faith are so closely linked that Joseph Smith spoke of working by faith as working by mental effort.

When a husband and a wife *think* together about the needs of their children, a certain kind of *synergism* develops in which their collective understanding is much greater than the sum of their individual understanding.

After our prayer that night we decided to begin an organized process of thinking about our children. We began to go on a special date together in the first week of every month. We went to a quiet restaurant and had a rule that we would discuss only one thing: our children. Over time, we began to call this monthly date discussion a "five-facet review" because we would ask each other, "How is Saren doing physically? mentally? emotionally? socially? spiritually?" We found that by asking these five questions about each child we could think thoroughly about each one. And we found, each time we had a "five-facet review," that we would discover a few specific things that needed our attention during the coming month.

We challenge you to adopt a similar pattern, even if you are just starting your family (in fact, *especially* if you are just starting). Get a special notebook and take it along with you each month to write down the conclusions and ideas that come to you.

There is a magical clarity and quality of insight that comes to parents as they *think* together about their children. Inspiration seems to follow, and the ideas they get and the conclusions they reach together are infinitely more valuable than any generalities they could gain from parenting books or "outside-the-family" sources.

Working with the Mind

It takes less calories by far,
so why
is it so much harder to think than to work?
"When a man works by faith," taught Joseph,
"he works by mental exertion."
It's easier to fix children a meal
than to think hard about their needs.
Easier to wash their clothes than to analyze them.
Easier to support them than to understand them.
Every answer we need
to serve our children is either in our mind or in
    God's.
We have access to both places,
but in sequence.
Searching our mind is called mental effort.
Searching his mind is called prayer.
Doing the first prepares us to do the second
Doing both makes us worthy stewards of God's
    children.

Lose Time Now, Gain It Later

The great French thinker and writer Rousseau said that "Parenting is the one profession in which we must learn how to lose time in order to gain it." One meaning, at least, is that if we can lose time *now* to our children to think of them, to listen to them, to serve them we will gain time in terms of how long we keep them, how long they trust us, how long our relationship with them lasts.

Here are three ways in which parents might "lose time":

> 1. *In thinking together with your spouse about your children.* In addition to the monthly five-facet review mentioned above, hold a weekly Sunday planning session.

Also, each night when you kneel to pray together, pause for a moment first (perhaps while already on your knees) to *think* about your children, their activities of that day, their needs. Your prayer will then include those needs and you will form a three-way partnership with God in your efforts to raise his children.

2. *In thinking within yourself about the kind of parent you want to be.* Pick out five characteristics that you believe would make you a better parent (such as patience, greater confidence in your children, calmness, and so on). Then pick an activity that you do every day (shaving, running, brushing teeth, anything that you do regularly that does not require conscious thought). Each day, during the activity you have chosen, remind yourself of the qualities of parenting you desire. Talk to yourself! Say, "I am a *patient* parent." Don't say, "I want to be patient." Decide that you *are* that quality now, and tell yourself so. Do it with each of the five qualities. This kind of self-programming can have amazing results. You will notice some changes in how you respond to your children within two or three weeks.

3. *In being with your children individually.* Regardless of how much time we spend in the same place as our children each day, we need to have certain times when we are totally *with* them, mentally as well as physically, when they have our total attention one at a time. We know one father who, at least four or five nights a week, insists on putting his small children to bed one at a time. He

asks if they had any "happies" or "sads" that day. He snuggles them. He is totally *with* them. Another father has an interview with each child each Sunday. He takes his children, one at a time, into his den and he listens. One mother with a large family of young children tries to take one of them on a "mommy date" each day. When her husband comes home from work he looks after the others while one child gets a few minutes of individual time with Mother.

Remember that time invested now brings great returns of time later. Small children are like fledgling businesses: They need large investments while they are little, and it is hard for a while to see their potential. When they grow, however, there are tremendous returns on those very early investments. In a business the return is money. In a family, the return is joy.

Prayer

We were trying to teach little three-year-old Jonah the reality of prayer one evening. We explained that he had two daddies and that the other one was up in heaven and could hear every word of his prayer. We told him how his Heavenly Daddy loved him with all his heart. We told him he could talk to that daddy just as he talked to his dad here on earth.

Jonah, whose gift is enthusiasm, got very excited. He had been saying little prayers for some time, but now he *really* wanted to talk "to his other daddy."

We knelt down together. Jonah, instead of looking down, looked *up,* and began, with a booming voice, "Hi, up there!"

Needless to say, our next discussion on prayer was about reverence and the use of proper words. But what a blessing it is to know God as a personal father! What a perspective to realize that we are his literal spirit children! Most prayerful people in the world call God "Father," but only we who have restored insight have the blessing of knowing that there is nothing figurative about that title.

In addition to teaching our children to pray and praying in our families, we need to pray as parents to our Father and seek earnestly his guidance and his knowledge of the children he has sent us. He knows them intimately and can be our source of understanding. After thinking about our children, we are in a position to say to the Lord, in essence, "Father, we have pondered and tried to know our children's needs. Wilt thou now further expand our minds and give us any additional insights necessary to raise them as thou wouldst have them raised."

We should also pray for our children's welfare, as did Alma, Sr., for Alma, Jr. (Mosiah 27:14). And we should remember and use our access to the most powerful kind of prayer we know, namely, priesthood blessings. The priesthood should be used often in our homes, not just in times of severe illness or crisis. When a child is afraid or deeply worried about something, when a family member has a big decision to make, when someone is trying to cope with a big problem of some kind, a priesthood blessing from Father is most appropriate. A great General Authority answered the question, "How can we have more spiritual experiences in our home?" by stating simply, "Use the priesthood more often."

15

Being a Child with Them

Grow Up—or Grow Down?

Did you ever consider how wrong it might be for a parent to say to a child, "Grow up," or "Act your age," or "Quit being such a child"? We would be better off if we said to ourselves, "Grow down," "Be more childlike," "Quit being such an adult."

Children are, in their natural state, magnificent creatures. They are filled with imagination, wonder, spontaneous delight, optimism, zest for life, trust, acceptance, forgiveness, hope, dreams, and love. Why would anyone want to change this? Rousseau said, "Hold childhood in reverence. Preserve its innocence and instinctive virtue."

Nothing gives a child more joy (and more *security*) than having a parent who, at least occasionally, will be a child with him. There are several ways to "grow down," each of which holds as much benefit for the parent as for the child.

Laughter

I (Richard) was in mainland China not too long ago, and on one bright autumn morning I got up long before our scheduled business meetings and found a taxi that was willing to take me out into the countryside. We went out to a small commune where most of the people had never seen a Caucasian (especially not a six-foot-four one wearing a silver jogging suit).

The Chinese are an open, unaffected, childlike people and they stared at me with open wonder. (I have since decided that many of them may have thought I was from a different planet.)

There was a small primary school in the little commune, and the tiny, black-eyed children were playing outside before class began. When I walked toward them they scattered like a flock of pigeons. I got down on one knee in an effort to look less threatening and one or two of the braver ones approached me, then curiosity overcame their fear. Then, like a returning flock, the others drifted and floated back toward me. I began to do some simple magic tricks and they soon crowded around with wide eyes and wide grins. In their faces was the universal peace and love of children. At one point I closed my eyes and listened to them laugh. I decided that the one truly universal language is children's laughter. It sounded just the same there, with my eyes closed, as my own children's laughter sounded eleven thousand miles away.

We parents don't laugh enough. Laughter is healthy, both mentally and physiologically. Doctors tell us that laughter causes a gastric secretion that aids digestion and is generally beneficial to our health.

As parents, we should strive to laugh more with our children. We should laugh at ourselves. G. K. Chesterton said the reason angels can fly is that they have learned to take themselves lightly.

We can think of funny things we did as children and tell them to our children—and laugh together. We can remember the principle that "crisis plus time usually equals humor."

One evening, a few years ago, everything had gone wrong at the Eyre house. *Every* child had spilled milk at dinner. The cat had dragged a dead bird into the house. Josh had broken a prong off the TV plug, so Dad had missed a special basketball game. Mom had lost a contact lens. Just when nothing else could possibly go wrong, little baby Saydi sitting in her high chair took her not-quite-empty soup bowl and turned it upside down on her head. We all laughed—and laughed, and laughed. The whole rotten day turned into humor; the tensions fled; we all felt better.

Lincoln once said, "Sometimes I am driven to my knees by the overwhelming conviction that I have nowhere else to go." We might reword that to say, "Sometimes in families we are driven to *laugh* by the overwhelming conviction that there is nothing else that can be done."

Imagination

With all the criticisms you have heard of television, let us add one more: It restricts the imagination. The images are already there for us. There is no mental work left to do, no need for imagination.

Our family spends much of each summer in a small cabin by a lake in Idaho, and one of its blessings is that there is no television. Imagination flourishes, even with Mom and Dad. We tell crazy stories and imagine wonderful things. We play games; we talk.

The children's favorite ongoing story is about the Do-little family, a family remarkably (in fact exactly) like ours who live in a place called "Mirrorland." In fact, any time you look into a mirror you see the corresponding member of the Dolittle family, and he is exactly like you except that he is left-handed and parts his hair on the opposite side. We tell stories about the future in the Dolittle family and we all imagine it with all our might.

Incidentally, we learned so much about the joys of no TV that ours is never turned on any more except on weekends. Instead, we try to get imagination to prevail. Characters vaguely resembling Daddy sometimes show up at bedtime. It might be "Polar Bear" in an old fur coat with a white ski mask, or "Monster Man" with a paper bag with eye holes, or even "Tinkerbell" with some kind of skirt and wig. All the characters live at the North Pole and are dispatched by Santa to visit children occasionally at bedtime and tell them a story or two. Tinkerbell sprinkles a little pixie dust on them and they fly directly to our house.

There is real joy in being a child with your small children and exercising your imaginations together. And there is even a sort of mysterious practicality. In the world we now live in, imagination and creative thinking are often the keys to success. And whatever it does for the children, imagination does a great deal for the uptight parents!

Spontaneity

We got home from a trip one evening and the baby-sitter already had the children in their pajamas. We were so happy to be together again that we just had to do something together before we put them to bed. One of the children wanted to go to the drive-in for a root beer. "But we'll have to get you dressed," we complained. "No, you won't," chimed in one of our more imaginative children. "*You* get on your pajamas and we'll all go like that." So we did.

Spontaneity is a gift of children and is too often lost by adults. We ought to try to recapture it whenever possible.

Childlike

Teach our children, we say.
Why?
It is they who have come recently from the
    heights.
They may not tell us with words of the other
    world,
but watch them,
for they know another language.
If we will put away our professional gowns
and take out our student pencil-pads,
and if we can shuck off the world
and its ridiculous notion
of "growing up,"
then they can teach us
of joy,
of peace,
of spontaneous delight.
They will let us back in
to that higher realm
called childhood.

Postscript

We all want life to be longer,
yet we're anxious to get each phase of life
out of the way.
We scramble toward *destinations:*
"When I arrive"
"Once I get there"
"When this is over"
"Just a little farther."
We are like rainbow-runners.
We imagine a pot of gold.
We forget that the rainbow itself is the reward.
There is no end,
there is no destination.
Even what we call celestial
is just another part of the trip.
What counts is the *journey*—
and what joy we find along the way.
Seek to slow time down, not speed it up.
Go especially slow when children are along,
for that is the trip's sweetest part.

16

Enjoying the Journey

"I Just Want to Get Off"

We took five of our children to Mexico not long ago, and at their request we went on a train from Nogales to Mazatlan. It seemed like a great idea until we got on. The trip took twenty hours. We were cramped together in a small Pullman compartment. The bunks were hard (and short). The train bounced and reeled like a drunken sailor. The toilet wouldn't flush. Jonah kept getting "car sick." It was almost funny, but not quite.

The worst part was getting off in Mazatlan and realizing that, in four days, we had to get back *on!*

The only difference on the return journey was that our car was the last one on the train. We wondered if we were just imagining that it was bouncier than on the way down, and then we remembered how, as children, we used to try to get in the last seat on the roller coaster, since that was where the "real action" was. The highlight of the return trip was when one bump dropped Daddy back onto his Pullman bunk so hard that his wind was knocked out.

Life is sometimes like a Mexican train ride. All we can think about is the destination. All we want to do is get off.

And yet in real life, in eternal life, there never really is a destination. We are on an eternal journey that leads us through endless phases of progression and growth.

It is ironic that all of us want our lives to be longer, yet we are always so anxious to get through the phase of life we are now in. We have a way of thinking that things will be better when we get that next promotion, or when we don't have children in diapers anymore, or when we retire, or when we get the children raised.

We need to realize that "to every thing there is a season," and that no time or season is inherently better or worse than any other. All are part of the journey. And the journey is to be enjoyed.

Two Goals

A father took his son on a hike. His goal was to get to the top of the plateau before dark so they could set up camp. He had underestimated the length of the hike and overestimated the speed and endurance of his son. It began to look as if they wouldn't make it. He prodded his boy, pushed him to go faster, got angry when the boy cried. He finally carried his son's pack along with his own, and in frustration almost dragged the upset little boy along. They finally did make it, just before dark, and succeeded in getting the camp set up.

Later on, as the boy slept, the father lay awake, staring up at the bright stars and realizing that he had put the wrong goal first. His real goal had been to enjoy his son, to talk together, to enjoy the journey. But the goal of getting there, of reaching the destination, had gotten in the way. He resolved to remember that, in all activities of life, there are two goals: (1) to get there, and (2) to enjoy the journey. He resolved to reverse their order in his mind.

May we as parents learn to enjoy the journey, and may we teach our children to do likewise.